From Seed to Harvest
Children's Agriculture Books

Speedy Publishing LLC
40 E. Main St. #1156
Newark, DE 19711
www.speedypublishing.com
Copyright 2016

All Rights reserved. No part of this book may be reproduced or used in any way or form or by any means whether electronic or mechanical, this means that you cannot record or photocopy any material ideas or tips that are provided in this book

How do plants grow? Have you watched them get taller and stronger?

Plants are a great attraction. They add beauty to our surroundings. They are one of nature's gifts to mankind.

Aside from being a beautiful sight, plants are very important to humans and animals. Animals eat plants to get energy. Moreover, humans eat plants and animals for energy, too!

Farmers work hard to grow crops on the farm to provide the needs of the people. The larger the harvest is, the more people are satisfied.

Plants are everywhere, but have you thought about what makes plants grow?

Growing plants either on a small garden or in the farm has always been a rewarding task.

Planting lets us experience the satisfaction that comes from caring for the seeds, then the seedlings and finally the adult plants. Observing how plants develop and grow is indeed very exciting.

Children who are involved in backyard gardening will have great chances of learning important life skills. Nurturing plants is a great way to learn skills and responsibility. Waiting for the plants to bear fruit requires patience.

Planting gives children a new way to explore nature. Hence, their environmental awareness is increased.

When the plants yield good results, the self-esteem of the children also grows. This helps them believe in their capabilities. Indeed, gardening is a fulfilling task.

Seeing a plant full of fruit is a great achievement for farmers. But what do plants need in order to grow and develop?

Plants are living things. They need sunlight, water, nutrients, air, and the appropriate temperature to survive and grow. If they survive and grow, they can reproduce.

Most plants grow from seeds. What happens when plants grow from seeds?

A seed contains an embryo inside it. The embryo contains the basic parts from which a seedling develops or grows. The seed itself contains food to keep the embryo alive until it can start to get nutrients from the soil.

The seed grows or sprouts in the right temperature. Seeds usually germinate in dark and damp conditions.

In order to survive, the seed absorbs water. When it is ready to greet the world, the case of the seed opens. As the seed breaks, roots of a new plant begin to grow. To help the plant stand, the roots grow downward and hold the plant in the soil while. For most plants the stem grows up toward the sun.

Eventually, shoots are seen above the ground and ready to straighten up and greet the sunlight. After several days, the plant develops and grows stems and leaves.

With continued care, the plants will bear flowers. Finally, the plants will grow fruits on their branches and stems, embedded among the leaves. Indeed, it is a marvelous plant life cycle.

Providing plants with proper nurturing helps make a good harvest.

Milton Keynes UK
Ingram Content Group UK Ltd.
UKHW052141230824
447186UK00004B/13